# Book of Poems From the Heart

**A Mother's Day Edition**

By
KIM GROSHEK

An imprint of Creatively Canny Publishing

Printed in the U.S.A.
ISBN-13: 978-1-942604-71-6

To all the poets, artists, and heart-driven catalysts—your voice matters, and your poem is within you. And to my daughter, always my heart.

# Foreword

There is a moment—a quiet, barely audible moment—when the heart speaks louder than the world around us. In that moment, we are called to pause. To listen. To feel. To remember who we are beneath the noise.

This book is born from those moments.

Each poem in these pages is a piece of my soul laid bare, an echo of lived experience, of deep love, of loss, of joy, of growth. They come not from a need to impress but from a need to express. To whisper truths that, too often, go unheard. To remind you, dear reader, that your feelings are valid, your story is sacred, and your voice—yes, *your* voice—matters.

*Book of Poems: From the Heart* is more than a collection of words. It is a companion. A mirror. A safe place to land when life feels heavy or when you simply need a nudge to remember your light.

As you turn each page, may you find pieces of yourself reflected here. May you be comforted, challenged, stirred, and inspired. And may you come back to this collection whenever your heart longs to be seen.

Thank you for walking this journey with me.

With a pause, with presence,
**Kim Groshek,** *Chief "Pause" Executive | Lifeful Habits*

# Preface

*From the Heart of Kim Groshek*

This book began as a whisper.
A whisper in the quiet corners of early mornings and long walks,
in the stillness between speaking engagements
and the hush before sleep.

A whisper that grew louder
each time I paused to listen—
not to the world,
but to the deep, steady rhythm of my own heart.

**Book of Poems: From the Heart** is the result of that listening.

These poems were written in moments of clarity and chaos,
joy and heartbreak, certainty and surrender.
They reflect the real and raw—
the human experience in its wholeness.

You will find here verses shaped by motherhood, legacy, courage, and longing.
By a deep knowing that within every one of us exists a story worthy of being heard.

This collection is not meant to be read in one sitting.
It's meant to be savored, returned to, like a letter from a dear friend.

Some pages may comfort you.
Others may stir something you've tucked away.
That's the beauty of poetry—
it speaks differently each time, depending on where your soul is standing.

Whether you are in a season of becoming, grieving, creating, healing, or simply being—this book is for you.

Thank you for allowing these words into your world.
May they meet you gently.

May they spark a pause.
May they awaken something beautifully true within you.

With love and light,
**Kim Groshek**, *The Pause Lady*

# Table of Contents

**Part I: The Quiet Beginnings** *Reflection, silence, and the foundation of inner strength.*

- The Pause
- Stillness
- Roots
- Listening
- The Language of Silence

**Part II: Fires of the Soul** *Passion, love, and the deep emotions that shape us.*

- Love Like a Wildfire
- Burning in the Depths
- Soul Mates
- The Silent Strength
- Courage, Wisdom & Grace

**Part III: The Heart That Breaks & Heals** *Loss, love, resilience, and the journey of healing.*

- A Mother's Wish
- The Gift of 'Ea'
- Never Alone
- Found
- You're Still Here
- The Storms of Love

**Part IV: Whispers of Light** *Inspiration, transformation, love, and the power of creation.*

- Love Like a Wildfire
- Soul Mates
- The Call to Create
- The First Steps
- Jamaica Morning
- Fail Big, Dream Bigger
- Whispers of Love
- Burning in the Depths of Diversity
- Aligned in Light
- A Mother's Wish

- Whisper of Grace
- The Silent Teacher
- 1000 Weekends
- The Gift of 'Ea'
- Wake Up, World
- Courage, Wisdom & Grace
- The Heart of It All
- Return to Gold
- Radiance
- Unlearning: 'Critical'
- Build a Fortress of Wonder: Bathe in Its Glory
- The Quiet Battle
- For When We Meet Again
- Whispers in Elixir: Chronicles of Peace

**Part V: Her Legacy** *Reflection, resilience, family, wisdom, and the passage of time.*

- Through Her Eyes
- In Her Footsteps
- A Prayer for Her Strength
- A Meditation for Her Love
- The Heartbeat of Us
- Her Journey
- There is a Truth
- Healing
- In the Chaos
- A Prayer Forgotten But Answered
- Generation Gaps
- A Mother's Heart
- Bridging Time: The Dance of Young Hearts and Old Souls
- Behind the Smile
- The Quirky Survivor
- Reach for the Sky
- The Silent Hero
- Song of Lost Time
- The Wild and the Wise
- Her Heart, Her World

- You’re Still Here
- Pancakes and Plans
- The Storms of Love
- Sisterhood in Summer
- Here
- Fragments of a Dream
- Breakfast Conversations
- A Message to My Son
- Between Sisters
- Ode to a Galaxy
- Hymn of Nature
- The Weight of Words
- Threads of Time

**Prayers & Meditations (Legacy & Reflection)**

- A Prayer for Her Peace
- A Meditation for Her Soul
- A Meditation for Her Journey
- A Prayer for Her Rest
- A Prayer for Her Courage
- A Meditation for Her Heart
- A Prayer for Her Peace of Mind
- A Meditation for Her Soul’s Purpose

**Closing Thoughts**

- The Strength We Share
- Hands That Hold
- In the Quiet of Our Hearts
- A Prayer for You, A Prayer for Me
- Space for Notes
- Epilogue
- With Love!

# Introduction

Words have always come to me—not in grand declarations but as gentle whispers from within. They arrive in pauses, breaths, and between life's beautiful chaos and quiet reflections. This collection is born from those sacred moments.

**Book of Poems: From the Heart** gathers emotions—truths I've lived, lessons learned, and stories that beg to be told in verse. Each poem is a thread woven into life's vibrant tapestry: the love of a mother, the ache of transformation, the fire of passion, the freedom of forgiveness, the courage to rise, and the call to pause.

This book isn't about perfection; it's about presence.

I invite you to read with an open heart. Let the words land where they may. Some will echo familiar feelings; others may gently awaken something new within you. That's the power of poetry—it meets us where we are and guides us where we need to go.

Feel free to read these poems sequentially or open to any page that calls to you. There's no right or wrong way—only your way.

My hope is that these pages create space for you—to feel, reflect, and reconnect. May you find moments of stillness, sparks of inspiration, and reminders that your story, too, is worth telling.

With all my heart,
**Kim Groshek,**
*The Pause Lady*

## *Part-1: The Quiet Beginnings*

## *The Pause*

*By Becky Allison*

I see glitter, shining in the sparkling air
I feel peaceful yet anxious at the same time.
I smell chocolate and coffee nearby

I taste my drink of pop and really don't want to cry.
I hear advice that I must take
So that I can relate to kids again and pause for them and for me.

## *Stillness*

*By Kim Groshek*

In the hush between heartbeats,
Where time pauses, suspended,
There lies a world untouched by chaos,
A realm where the soul is mended.
The gentle sway of ancient trees,
Whispering secrets of the past,
Their leaves dance in silent symphony,
In rhythms that forever last.
The vast expanse of star-strewn skies,
Infinite in their serene grace,
Invite the mind to wander freely,
To find its quiet resting place.
In stillness, we uncover truths,
Hidden beneath life's clamor and din,
A sanctuary for the weary,
A path that leads the soul within.
So, pause amidst your hurried steps,
Embrace the calm, the peace, the rest,
For in the quiet, we discover
The essence of our very best.

## *Art is a Revolution*

*By Kim Groshek*

They told us art was a luxury,
a side note, a quiet thing.
But we know better.
Art is fire.

Art is rebellion.
Art is the battle cry of the ones who refuse to be tamed.
Ink on skin, paint on walls,
poetry spit like gunfire into the night—

this is how we rise.
This is how we take back what was stolen.
No apologies. No hesitation.
We create because we must.

So tell me, will you shape the world with your hands?
Will you carve light into the dark?
Will you stand at the edge and scream—
I AM HERE. I AM ALIVE. I WILL CREATE.

## *Butterfly Grandma's Story*

<u>Song 1</u> & <u>Song 2</u>
*By Kim Groshek*

I sit so still, my hands in my lap,
Listening close to the softest of chat.
Grandma weaves a tale in the air,
A story of change, beyond all compare.

"Grandma, why do you love them so?"
I ask, my voice quiet, gentle, and low.
She smiles, her eyes like the morning light,
Holding the wisdom of stars at night.

"My dear," she whispers, touching my hand,
"A caterpillar crawls on earth's warm sand.
Small and plain, it knows not yet,
The wings of wonder it will get."

"It weaves a home, a silent shell,
A sacred space where dreams will swell.
It waits, it shifts, it breaks, it flies—
A miracle born before our eyes."

I see her smile, soft and bright,
Her heart alight with golden light.
And in that moment, I understand,
The magic she holds in her weathered hand.

* * *

For we, too, grow—we shed, we break,
We pause, we change, we rise awake.
And just like wings so bold, so free,
We become all we're meant to be.

## *A Mother's Heart*

*By Kim Groshek*

In her eyes, a gentle spark,
Guiding you from light to dark.
Through each step, she softly bends,
A mother's love, it never ends.

She lifts you high, she holds you near,
Whispers words that calm your fear.
Her embrace, a constant guide,
No distance too great, no wave too wide.

Through every storm, she stands so tall,
A steady hand through life's great call.
Her strength is built of love and grace,
A mother's heart, no one can replace.

With each new dawn, her love renews,
A bond that time can never bruise.
Through laughter, tears, and every fight,
She loves you deep, with all her might.

# *Part-2: Fires of the Soul*

## *A Mother's Prayer*

*By Kim Groshek*

In the quiet of the night, she prays,
For strength and courage through your days.
With every hope, she lets you fly,
But keeps her dreams beside you, nigh.

She prays for peace within your soul,
For wisdom to help you reach your goal.
Her silent prayers rise up so high,
A mother's love that can never die.

Through every tear, she holds you near,
Her voice a calm, your heart sincere.
She trusts the path that you must take,
Her prayer the spark that helps you wake.

And when you face the world so wide,
She'll stand with you, right by your side.
For in her prayer, you'll always find,
A mother's love, pure and kind.

## *Eviction*

*By London Forbes*

They say love feels like coming home,
But you taught me homes foreclose—
That forever arrives stamped
With an eviction date.

# *The Freedom of Release*

*by Kim Groshek*

The storms inside are not my war,
I carry them, but they don't define,
When I release what's not my core,
The storm and I become aligned.

Cancel culture's noise is loud,
Judgment viral, deep as breath,
But I stand unshaken, proud,
For I hold my truth, defying death.

I take nothing personally,
And that, my friends, is power's key,
The secret's simple: to be free,
Is to let go and just *be me*.

'ea, the wisdom in my veins,
A gift that cuts through all the lies,
In standing true, the storm remains,
But my soul forever flies.

## *Unveiled*

*By Kim Groshek*

I spent so long behind a mask,
Smiling, nodding—playing the task.
A perfect image, built so tight,
But inside, I feared the light.

I counted flaws, I cursed my frame,
Never enough, drowning in shame.
The world saw strong, but I knew weak,
A hollow shell, afraid to speak.

But then He came—no shame, no blame,
Just love that called me by my name.
He took my hand, He met my eyes,
And suddenly, I recognized—

I was His. I was free.
No need to hide the real me.
I stand unveiled, no chains, no lies,
A daughter of God—redeemed, alive.

## *A Mother's Song*

*By Kim Groshek*

She hums a song you can't forget,
A melody of love, no regret.
Through every note, she sings so sweet,
A mother's love, forever neat.

Her song is one of quiet grace,
A soothing tune, a warm embrace.
In every line, you feel her care,
A mother's love, beyond compare.

Through every struggle, every fight,
Her song will bring you back to light.
She sings the words you cannot see,
A mother's love, a melody.

And as you grow, you'll sing along,
The very tune of her sweet song.
For in her voice, you'll always know,
A love that helps your heart to grow.

## *A Mother's Love and a Daughter's Pain are One in the Same*

*By Maresa Roach*

A young girl all alone in the world. With no one to love. I can imagine she wishes she looked above. Above, to the one that gives life without condemnation or strife.

Our Father, God above you, would give you love. But instead, you turned to my father. Who departed life before I was born. Oh, how you must've been torn and filled with scorn.

You did your part right from the start. During my conception, you fought depression but refused to give up. You thought you were alone and didn't realize God looked high and low on his throne. He had you in his hand; despite how you felt, he had a master plan.

Born in a Catholic hospital, they considered it a sin. For a single woman to give birth without being married. But you carried me for nine months. The nurse asked, "Do you want to give her up for adoption?"

"No," you replied. "I don't want to give my baby away." You chose me and didn't think twice because you gave me life. How could you possibly win and give in to the thought of another family taking me in?

Loving you from a heart of hurt. Often misunderstood. We had growing pains due to our disdain. Our hearts and souls are bold through our story of hurt and pain. But we realized we are the same.

We have reclaimed what was lost. We will be together until we depart. You will always be in my heart. Above all else, guard your heart, For everything you do flows from it. **Proverbs 4:23 (NIV)**

## *The Unseen Strength*

*By Kim Groshek*

She wakes before the sun's first light,
Chasing dreams that feel out of sight.
With coffee in hand and kids in tow,
She's balancing worlds they'll never know.

A smile on her lips, though tired eyes,
She hides her struggles, never cries.
With every task, she pushes through,
Juggling all, while staying true.

Her heart's a well, so deep and wide,
It holds the love she can't hide.
Through all the chaos, she stands tall,
The unseen strength that carries it all.

Though she doesn't ask for much in return,
Her love's the flame that'll always burn.
She's the backbone, the quiet force,
That keeps her world on its true course.

## *Never Alone*

*By Anna L. Lewis*

Feelings of loneliness and despair
A crowd surround me
But it's like no one's there
Forcing my way

Pushing through the crowd
The noise loud
Every direction pulling
Ripping me to threads

I hear you but I don't hear you
It's like no one's there
If I can just get past the
Distractions of the past

Hindering, stagnating
My growth
If I can just focus my ear
That one voice I would hear

Clearly
But I'm pushing my way
Through
God, I need to see you

Hear you

Touch the hem of your garment
Every step brings me closer
Softer the noise

Clearer your voice
Closer the hem
As my head bows low.....
I see footsteps follow my every move

Could it be you?
I'm encouraged
I was never alone
You walked me through the storms

Never left my side
Please be my guide
As I traverse the unknown
For with you, I'm never alone

## *Called by Name*

*By Kim Groshek*

Through the chaos, through the noise,
I hear His voice, a quiet choice.
Not demanding, not unkind,
Just a whisper in my mind.

"Come to me, let go, be still,
Trust the path, embrace My will."
Doubt dissolves, the fear departs,
Peace now pulses in my heart.

I am known, I am free,
Not just me—but Christ in me.
A guiding light, a sacred flame,
Walking forward, called by name.

## *Endless Rewinds*

*By Kim Groshek*

She doesn't get a pause, a break,
Yet still, she gives for everyone's sake.
Her mind rewinds with every day,
Chasing moments that slip away.

She's the glue, holding it together,
She'll keep it strong through any weather.
Her heart beats fast, but never loud,
A quiet queen beneath the crowd.

The weight she carries no one sees,
Yet she wears it with such ease.
Her sacrifice is just her way,
Of loving others through the fray.

Still, she wonders if anyone knows,
That beneath her strength, her heart glows.
A mother's love, both fierce and kind,
Endless rewinds, never far behind.

## *That's What I Learned V1*

*By Kim Groshek*

That's what I learned—
that if you're going to be brave,
you're going to fall.

It's not the critic who counts.
It's not the man who points out how the strong man stumbles
or where the doer of deeds could have done it differently.

The credit belongs to the person who's actually in the arena,
whose face is marred with sweat and dust and blood,
who strives valiantly,
who comes up short again and again and again,

who in the end may know the triumph of high achievement,
and who, when he fails,
he does so daring greatly.

That's what I learned—
that if you're going to be brave,
you're going to fall.

## *The Brave and the Fall*

*By Kim Groshek*

If you choose to be bold, to stand tall,
Know this truth—you're bound to fall.
Not the critic, not their gaze,
Not the one who points and weighs.

Not the voice that mocks defeat,
Calling where the strong man's weak.
Not the one who claims to see
How the doer should have been free.

The praise belongs to those who fight,
Who step into the harshest light.
Face streaked with sweat, with dust, with blood,
Still they rise from every flood.

They strive, they fall, they rise once more,
They knock, they push on every door.
And though they lose, though stakes run steep,
They fall with courage, fierce and deep.

For in the end, the great ones know,
It's through the falls that strength will grow.
So if you're brave, then take the call—
Step ahead—yes, you may fall.

## *A Love Unbroken*

*By Joanne B Lewis*

"We lived thirty-nine years together, being sista friends and loving one another. We met one Sunday at church. I had no idea when my daughter and I sat down, that the two women sitting behind us would become part of our family.

It was really God that forged our relationships, from our first time sharing a good morning smile. Our mothers would become friends, our children, our extended families, friends definitely knew we had one another's backs, we prayed for and with one another, respected and loved each other.

Our sista love was real, we lived through different life events and phases. We were like two teenage girls, giggling, laughing, sharing secrets, secrets that we knew were seared into our bond.

Before we each got married, the fiancés received a very stern warning, from our mothers and each other. They were told that "as long as my sister is happy and you take more than excellent care of her, then you would not have any problems or bodily harm affected!" We were serious too!

We went to concerts, the opera, we took advantage of all types of dining, and of course we loved to shop together or online. The experience was golden; we had sophisticated shopping skills. We definitely enjoyed going out to eat, she took forever to decide what she would order and even longer eating her food. I would ask her, "why is it taking you so long to eat?" Her response, "you know" and then she'd give me that smile. She always wanted to take something sweet home.

We shared our love for Franciscan China, she had Desert Rose, I have the Apple design. We absolutely treasured our china and talked about how there was no need to save them for a special occasion, we were purposely living each day as best as we could, within our humanness.

We shared humorous events of bra shopping, we swapped stories of our experiences and then fell out laughing and crying, we could not help ourselves.

We were sisters, always there for one another, understanding quiet times, times when words were not enough. We shared our happy, joyful times, the times when death and grief consumed us, our mothers passing a year within one another. We understood the darkness of grief, the hopelessness of your heart wanting what God will not permit, the need to bargain with God, to bring our mothers back to us, or take us to be with them.

We were not naïve, we knew we could not bargain with God, it did not stop the grief and darkness, the beauty of it all is that we knew we had one another. I am thankful for her presence in my life forever. I ended each phone call with "I love you always," she would say, "I love you too and we will talk soon."

I will always love and miss my bestest sista friend. Please, kiss our mommies and everybody for me, love you always."

# *Part-3: The Heart That Breaks & Heals*

## *A Journey Through Myth and Magic*

*By Kim Groshek*

Through wardrobe's door and forest deep,
Where Aslan's roar makes shadows creep,
A golden road winds far and wide,
Past rolling hills where secrets hide.

A silver ring, both dark and bright,
Whispers fate in morning's light.
Yet far away, beyond the mist,
A wizard waits with clenched-tight fist.

A scarecrow bows, his mind now keen,
A tin man longs for things unseen.
A cowardly lion, bold yet torn,
Finds his roar where myths are born.

Through emerald gates and towers tall,
Through Middle-earth where echoes call,
Through Narnian seas and lands untold,
Their fates entwine in threads of gold.

For wisdom grows where hearts are tried,
And power bends to those denied.
But in the end, one truth remains—
A heart of courage breaks the chains.

## *1000 Weekends*

*By Paul Osterhout*

I have 1000 weekends left to live,
A thousand moments, still to give.
Friday nights to gently unwind,
From the week's work, to peace of mind.

A thousand Saturdays to rise,
With new adventures in our eyes.
Mornings filled with endless chance,
To laugh, to love, to dance the dance.

A thousand Sundays, soft and slow,
To pause, reflect, and gently grow.
To reset dreams, to plan anew,
For all the days we'll journey through.

These numbers finite, yet so bright,
Reminders in the soft twilight.
Each weekend holds a gift, a chance,
For memories made in life's dance.

Not a countdown, but a climb,
To cherish every passing time.
Fridays are for joy's sweet song,
Saturdays for hearts made strong.

Sundays bring a quiet grace,

To ready for the next embrace.
It's quality that makes life shine,
Not numbers on a finite line.

A thousand weekends, gifts they are,
To reach, to dream, to travel far.
Let's count not down, but up with glee,
To love, to grow, to simply be.

The real treasure, not in sum,
But in each moment's welcome drum.
Embrace each weekend with intent,
For life is best when well-spent.

## *The Quiet Power*

*by Kim Groshek*

In a world that spins on whispers,
I've learned the art of silence,
Not the kind that buries the voice,
But the kind that holds the balance.

I don't need to prove my worth,
I don't need to show my flame,
For I am the fire and the earth,
Unshaken by the winds of shame.

**Two letters** change the game,
*No* to the chaos, *yes* to the calm,
I take nothing personally,
For peace lives within the palm.

In the theater of light and shadow,
Where others wear their rage,
I stand unshaken, letting go,
Of what's not mine to cage.

## *The Silent Strength*

*By Kim Groshek*

She doesn't ask for praise or fame,
Her heart a fire, a burning flame.
She gives without a thought of return,
Her love a lesson you will learn.

Her strength is silent, yet so loud,
She walks among the bustling crowd.
Her love surrounds, a steady force,
Guiding you back to the right course.

Through all the years, through joy and strife,
She shapes the world, she shapes your life.
Her love will carry, always near,
A mother's strength, forever clear.

And when you feel like you've lost your way,
She'll be the light to guide your stay.
Her strength, a beacon in the dark,
A mother's love, a constant spark.

## *The Echo of Now*

*By Linda Thuy Le*

I run, I chase, I dream of more,
Tomorrow calls, so much in store!
I long to grow, to touch the sky,
Why must time crawl, not fly?

I run, I chase, I count the days,
Caught in the doing, lost in the maze.
Deadlines, dishes, tasks in line,
How can I pause? There's never time.

I sit, I smile, I watch them go,
The rush of youth, the weary flow.
I tried to grasp, to hold, to claim,
But seasons pass, we're all the same.

Oh, child so eager, let wonder stay.
Oh, parent so burdened, see today.
Oh, elder so wise, in rest abide,
For love is here, not far, not wide.

But when I'm grown, then I'll be free!
The world will bow and notice me.
If only I had one more hour…
To hear the laughter, smell the flowers.

I had it all, I see it now,

The magic was here, in the now.
So lift your eyes, unbend your hands,
Step out from time's unyielding sands.

For love was never then or when,
It's only now, again, again.
I ran, I chased, I touched the sun,
And only now, I see, I'd won.

Not in the race, not in the climb,
But in the breath between the time.
I built, I toiled, I shaped a life,
A mother, father, husband, wife.

But love, I see, is never stored,
It lives when freely given more.
I watched, I wept, I let things go,
A tide that pulls, a quiet flow.

Regret? Perhaps. But this I know:
Fear dims the light; let go, and glow.
Oh, child who longed for what's ahead,
Oh, parent tangled in the thread,

Oh, elder looking back so far,
The gift was always where you are.
So hear me now, before time shifts,
Before the sand no longer drifts.

The purpose here was never race,
Nor wealth, nor time, nor fleeting chase.
It's love.
It's presence.

It's hand in hand.
It's knowing now,
Not when you've planned.
So stop,

And feel,

See, and be.
For love is now,
For love is free.

So whether you run or rest,
Whether you chase or wait,
Whether you want or wish,
Whether you reach for what was or ache for what will be,

This moment is all you will ever have.
So stop. Breathe.
Take in the whisper of the wind, the warmth of the sun,
The laughter, the sorrow, the clinking of dirty dishes,

These small, fleeting, imperfect joys are your life.
Do not rush to the last page and leave the middle unwritten.
No one else is holding the pen but you.
For you will rush to the end, only to wish you could do it all over again.

## *A Mother's Prayer*

*By Kim Groshek*

In the quiet of the night, she prays,
For strength and courage through your days.
With every hope, she lets you fly,
But keeps her dreams beside you, nigh.

She prays for peace within your soul,
For wisdom to help you reach your goal.
Her silent prayers rise up so high,
A mother's love that can never die.

Through every tear, she holds you near,
Her voice a calm, your heart sincere.
She trusts the path that you must take,
Her prayer the spark that helps you wake.

And when you face the world so wide,
She'll stand with you, right by your side.
For in her prayer, you'll always find,
A mother's love, pure and kind.

## *Eviction*

*By London Forbes*

They say love feels like coming home,
But you taught me homes foreclose—
That forever arrives stamped
With an eviction date.

## *The Freedom of Release*

*by Kim Groshek*

The storms inside are not my war,
I carry them, but they don't define,
When I release what's not my core,
The storm and I become aligned.

Cancel culture's noise is loud,
Judgment viral, deep as breath,
But I stand unshaken, proud,
For I hold my truth, defying death.

I take nothing personally,
And that, my friends, is power's key,
The secret's simple: to be free,
Is to let go and just *be me*.

'ea, the wisdom in my veins,
A gift that cuts through all the lies,
In standing true, the storm remains,
But my soul forever flies.

## *Through Her Eyes*

*By Kim Groshek*

In her eyes, you'll see your worth,
A love that gives you endless birth.
She watches as you grow and rise,
Her love reflected in your eyes.

Through every storm, she stands with you,
Her faith in you, pure and true.
Her lessons deep, her heart so kind,
A mother's love, you'll always find.

Through triumphs and through days of rain,
She teaches how to love through pain.
Her hands, though worn, will never tire,
Her love will always lift you higher.

And when you leave, her love stays near,
A quiet force, a voice so clear.
Through her eyes, you'll always see,
A mother's love, eternally.

## *What Will Be Your Something More?*

*By Alicia Pozsony*

I awake and see
the sun and sky above me
I rise, yet I cannot resonate
feel the words within ache

I question everything
Purpose for every being
Yet, why is it so hard?
fear, limits our reward

Searching, seeking, dreaming for more
Patience, yearning, counting the score
I put the work in
to study and learn, I bend

when will I feel longings end?
Shadows of my mistakes plague me
to face them is the only way to flee
Another day, I rise

the sun and sky above me
so is my growing confidence so lovely
I see differently now
the path is clear

no judgment, limits or fear

experience has taught
resilience has brought
the joy I once sought

hope remains
the day regains
the love and light shines bright
my day may end

but my night is still bright
I can lead my path to free
and live a life that is meant to be
I can rise and resonate

I can strive to be something great
So can you—
Catch your destiny before it's too late
Our journey path is not straight

with faith you can elevate
A leader—
Smart, Fierce, Caring and Kind
My life is not to be lived in rewind

I focus on the people who need me
to create a better world bravely
No excuses, no limits this hour
My story is my power

Every day you rise
like the sun and skies
Stand tall, be great
Rise & Resonate for your something more!

## *From Darkness to Light*

*By Kim Groshek*

For years, I walked with my head held low,
A stranger to myself, afraid to show.
Mirrors whispered lies, shadows grew tall,
I shrank, I hid—I lost it all.

I called it strength, this silent fight,
But I was drowning in the night.
Hating, running, numb to grace,
Afraid to even see my face.

But He was there—He never left,
Through every wound, through every breath.
A whisper broke the chains I wore,
A light poured through an open door.

Now I rise, now I see,
I was never lost—He carried me.
No more fear, no more shame,
I stand in love, He calls my name.

## *The Silent Strength of a Mother's Love*

*By Kim Groshek*

Her power lies in quiet grace,
A mother's love, no time can erase.
She watches as you spread your wings,
And smiles through every joy it brings.

Her sacrifices, not always seen,
But in her heart, they're evergreen.
She builds your world with every word,
A silent strength, never deterred.

Through days of joy, through nights of fear,
She's always there, always near.
Her love a fortress, pure and bright,
Guiding you through dark and light.

And when you stumble, when you fall,
Her love will answer, her arms will call.
For in a mother's gentle power,
She's your safe place in every hour.

## *Unveiled*

*By Kim Groshek*

I spent so long behind a mask,
Smiling, nodding—playing the task.
A perfect image, built so tight,
But inside, I feared the light.

I counted flaws, I cursed my frame,
Never enough, drowning in shame.
The world saw strong, but I knew weak,
A hollow shell, afraid to speak.

But then He came—no shame, no blame,
Just love that called me by my name.
He took my hand, He met my eyes,
And suddenly, I recognized—

I was His. I was free.
No need to hide the real me.
I stand unveiled, no chains, no lies,
A daughter of God—redeemed, alive.

## *Something Happened to Me*

*By Marco Islas*

Something happened to me. It's hard to explain, Yes life happens-yes everyone goes through things- but damn-Something happened to me-I need to let it out.

I've known pain. Pain you can probably relate to, I've been hurt before

I was hit off my motorcycle-hit and run, I broke my face on a metal bar at 20 mph, At 17 my pregnant gf told me our child, might not be mine-might,

Yet, this isn't it- not what happened to me-Something happened to me-I never knew this pain before-did not know this much existed-it came like a thief in the cover of dark-it broke me-a million, pieces-never thought I could be whole again. Ready to not exist. Yet- here I am. Here with YOU. Phoenix out of the ashes. Better than ever.

Something happened to me-life from a different lens. So yeah, anyone can come at me with anger, apathy, excuses- All of it- In the end, it doesn't matter. No one can take anything from me, I'm past all of that-I'm here to live-Something happened to me, I'm different now.

## *Found*

*By Kim Groshek*

I used to run from my own reflection,
A life of shame, a disconnection.
I built my walls, I closed my heart,
Convinced that love was not my part.

But grace pursued—so wild, so true,
It shattered all I thought I knew.
Not in thunder, not in flame,
But in the whisper of my name.

He saw the parts I tried to hide,
The years I fought, the tears I cried.
Yet still, He called, yet still, He stayed,
His love refused to turn away.

Now I see what He has known,
I was never meant to be alone.
From dark to light, from lost to found,
I stand in Him—on solid ground.

## *A Mother's Song*

*By Kim Groshek*

She hums a song you can't forget,
A melody of love, no regret.
Through every note, she sings so sweet,
A mother's love, forever neat.

Her song is one of quiet grace,
A soothing tune, a warm embrace.
In every line, you feel her care,
A mother's love, beyond compare.

Through every struggle, every fight,
Her song will bring you back to light.
She sings the words you cannot see,
A mother's love, a melody.

And as you grow, you'll sing along,
The very tune of her sweet song.
For in her voice, you'll always know,
A love that helps your heart to grow.

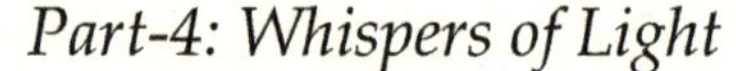

*Part-4: Whispers of Light*

## *Divine Reflection*

*By Kim Groshek*

I search for You in winds that blow,
In rushing streams, in peaks of snow.
Yet You are here, so close, so near,
Not in the sky, but deep and clear.

A mirror held, I see Your face,
Love and wisdom, endless grace.
Not apart, but whole, in sync,
Your thoughts are mine, the missing link.

No more seeking far and wide,
You are here, You live inside.
Higher self, divine embrace,
Every breath—a gift of grace.

## *Love Like a Wildfire*

*By Kim Groshek*

Love me like the sun setting itself on fire,
like a storm tearing through the quiet sky,
like a revolution that never stops burning.
Give me the reckless, the unapologetic,

the love that doesn't ask for permission.
Hold nothing back.
No half-measures. No maybe laters.
Love me like the artists love their madness,

like the dreamers chase their stars,
like the universe expands—
without fear, without limit, without end.
Because anything less isn't love.

It's just waiting.
And I was never meant to wait.

## *Soul Mates*

*By Veronika Peña de la Jara*

I thought I would find you,
Come across you, see you someday.
I thought that through my eyes I would recognize who you were;
Now I understand that you are nowhere.

That when I close my own eyes
Look within
That is where I find you.
I always thought that when I kissed you

Tasted you, absorbed you someday.
I thought the chemistry in me, would recognize the chemistry in you; -
Now I understand you are nowhere.
It is here

As I taste my own flesh
That I find you.
I always thought that when you'd touch me
And my body quivered
Beneath your tender fingertips, I would know an angel was holding me;

Now I understand that when I feel into my own body,
acknowledge my own quiveryness
That I find you,
in the end.

* * *

You are within me.
The moment I chose to be present
Accepting and here in this moment, in the world around me,
That is where you reside.

There is the company I always sought
You're here with me.
When they say love yourself,
What they mean is;

Love this moment
And yourself in it.
Be here.
With gratitude in your eyes, a sweet taste in your mouth

Centered in your body;
And understand that this is it.
This is life.
This is here and now.

This is, my friend,
This is where your soulmate lies.

## *The Call to Create*

*By Kim Groshek*

I stand at the edge, toes curled over infinity,
the abyss hums beneath me—electric, alive.
I do not flinch.
I do not step back.
I cry out—
for the wild ones, the fearless, the dreamers,
for the artists who carve light from shadow,
who dare to shape the unseen.
I offer no gold, no false promises,
only the truth—
your art is a revolution,
a pulse in the dark.
Would you dare?
Would you create for nothing but belief?
No safety net. No reward.
Just the raw, beating force of inspiration,
the wild call of something greater—
a truth too loud to ignore.
Stand with me.
Paint the sky with me.
Sing the song that has never been sung.
For artistry. For love. For community.
For the psychedelic echo that reminds us—
we are infinite.

## *The First Steps*

*By Kim Groshek*

You took your first steps in her arms,
A world of wonder, free from harm.
She held your hand, you felt her trust,
And slowly, surely, grew from dust.

Through scraped knees and whispered pain,
She showed you how to rise again.
With every fall, you learned to stand,
Her love forever, your guiding hand.

Her voice a melody, soft and clear,
Teaching you the way, year by year.
Through every challenge, she's by your side,
A mother's love, her heart your guide.

And though you soar, her wings still near,
A love unbroken, always here.
From first steps to dreams you chase,
She's proud of every leap you take.

## *Jamaica Morning*

*By Julia JonesBrown*

I see the life continuing below.
I feel the tingling sensation of the wind tickling my sun-kissed skin.
I hear the birds chirping, while tasting the salty fresh dew from the break of dawn.

## *Fail Big Dream Bigger*

*By Kim Groshek*

Fail big fall flat on your face
Feel the fire of a boundless space
Every scar's just a map to gold
Every story's worth being told
Dream bigger break through the height
Run to the edge chase the light
They'll call you mad they'll call you wild
But that's where the giants smiled
Face the doubt like a roaring wind
Catch the future let the games begin
Step to the rhythm don't fear the fall
It's your chance to claim it all
Dream bigger break through the height
Run to the edge chase the light
They'll call you mad they'll call you wild
But that's where the giants smiled
Let them point let them scorn and tease
Let them sneer while you defy the breeze
You're not built for the quiet or the small
You are fire rise above them all
Dream bigger break through the height
Run to the edge chase the light
They'll call you mad they'll call you wild
But that's where the giants smiled

## *Whispers of Love*

*By Kim Groshek*

Song 2

In the quiet of the night,
She whispers love with all her might.
A lullaby for dreams to grow,
A love so deep, you'll always know.

Through sleepless nights and endless care,
She's always there, she's always fair.
Her hands may tire, her heart still strong,
She hums the tune of right and wrong.

Her love's a blanket, soft and warm,
A shield that keeps you safe from storm.
No matter where the road may roam,
Her love will always guide you home.

And when you fly, she'll wave goodbye,
But in her heart, you'll never die.
A mother's love will never part,
It's etched forever on her heart.

*Burning in the Depths of Diversity*

*By Rebecca Engle*

Born with a voice the world couldn't hear,
Silent whispers, a quiet fear.
Words were locked, just out of sight,
Yet her mind burned bold and bright.

Letters danced but wouldn't stay,
Sounds that tangled, slipped away.
Still, she fought, step by stride,
With a fire she kept inside.

Educational meetings, goals in place,
Marked her path, set the pace.
Teachers wondered, doubted too,
But she knew what she could do.

A turning point, a shift, a spark,
Her silence fading in the dark.
From nonverbal, she took flight,
Found her strength, found her light.

Books and lessons, years went fast,
Proving limits don't hold fast.
College halls, a master's plan,
Leading, teaching, taking a stand.

Now she lifts the ones who wait,

For words to form, for paths to shape.
IEP pages, goals to write,
Giving kids their voice, their right.

An author, teacher, advocate strong,
She turns struggle into song.
For every child who's told "not yet,"
She's the proof—don't you forget.

## *Aligned in Light*

*By Kim Groshek*

I close my eyes, the world fades dim,
A quiet voice, a call from Him.
Not in thunder, not in flame,
But in love—He speaks my name.

No rush, no fear, no need to run,
Just stillness with the Holy One.
A breath, a pause, a soul set free,
His grace unfolding inside me.

I lay my burdens, shed the weight,
Step in faith—no need to wait.
A whisper guides, a light breaks through,
Truth so clear, so deep, so true.

I rise, I walk, my heart now whole,
Christ within—the fire, the soul.
No longer lost, no longer blind,
I am His, and He is mine.

## *A Mother's Wish*

*By Lisa Burns*

Beautiful daughter you were almost ten,
When I left you on that winter day.
You see my beauty, your eyes did not know,
Even until this day how sad to say,

It was for me to stay.
Pain inside, unseen to the naked eye,
Cries for change without condemnation.
So be it NOT to be,

For there are far more stories to uncover to be certain,
I did it for the love of your heart and your other two sisters.
They have forgiven me since.
You are not so much.

Your forgiveness remains locked within.
One day as we know it,
There will come a time of understanding and growth for both of us
but,
For now, we have, or I do that is…

To simply wait and have faith in the power to heal
and be happy with truth as the guide towards you.

## *Whisper of Grace*

*By Kim Groshek*

In the hush before the dawn,
I feel His presence—gentle, strong.
Not in noise, not in might,
But in the stillness, pure and bright.

A whisper calls, my spirit stirs,
Love so vast, no need for words.
I lift my hands, my heart takes flight,
Wrapped in mercy, bathed in light.

No more striving, no more fear,
His voice is calm, His path is clear.
I am known, I am free,
Christ within, alive in me.

## *The Silent Teacher*

*By Kim Groshek*

In moments when words cannot speak,
She shows you all you need to seek.
Her wisdom flows like rivers wide,
Her lessons taught without pride.

In her smile, you find your way,
A guiding light throughout each day.
Her quiet strength, a lesson learned,
Her heart, the place where dreams are turned.

Through every trial, she's still the one,
The silent teacher, never undone.
With gentle eyes, she helps you grow,
A love that never lets you go.

Her hands may tremble, but she'll hold,
A mother's love, a story bold.
In her embrace, you find your ground,
In her, a strength that will resound.

## *1000 Weekends*

*By Paul Osterhout*

I have 1000 weekends left to live,
A thousand moments, still to give.
Friday nights to gently unwind,
From the week's work, to peace of mind.

A thousand Saturdays to rise,
With new adventures in our eyes.
Mornings filled with endless chance,
To laugh, to love, to dance the dance.

A thousand Sundays, soft and slow,
To pause, reflect, and gently grow.
To reset dreams, to plan anew,
For all the days we'll journey through.

These numbers finite, yet so bright,
Reminders in the soft twilight.
Each weekend holds a gift, a chance,
For memories made in life's dance.

Not a countdown, but a climb,
To cherish every passing time.
Fridays are for joy's sweet song,
Saturdays for hearts made strong.

Sundays bring a quiet grace,

To ready for the next embrace.
It's quality that makes life shine,
Not numbers on a finite line.

A thousand weekends, gifts they are,
To reach, to dream, to travel far.
Let's count not down, but up with glee,
To love, to grow, to simply be.

The real treasure, not in sum,
But in each moment's welcome drum.
Embrace each weekend with intent,
For life is best when well-spent.

## *The Gift of 'Ea"*

*by Kim Groshek*

From these words to my heart,
A wisdom ancient and pure,
'*ea' whispered a truth so sharp,
It cut through noise, secure.

In this life, we're told to fight,
To defend, to prove, to chase,
But 'ea' taught me there's more light,
In standing still, in finding grace.

The elders knew what we forget,
That power's never a fight,
It's owning what we can't regret,
And letting go of borrowed might.

Not to compare, but to honor—
Our gifts, like stars in endless sky,
Sovereignty is the light I offer,
A birthright, no need to vie.

## *Wake Up, World*

*By Kim Groshek*

Eyes half-open, stretch, then blink,
Sunlight creeping—time to think.
Phone still silent, world so still,
One deep breath—I catch the thrill.

Feet hit floor, no rush, no race,
Just me, this moment, time, and space.
Coffee brews, the day's brand new,
What's the move? What's the view?

No autopilot, no rewind,
Just today—this state of mind.
I shake the sleep, I claim the spark,
Step outside, embrace the dark.

Sky turns colors, air feels light,
Fresh starts brewing—yeah, that's right.
No past to chase, no fear to keep,
Just waking up—no need to leap.
But I will.

## *Courage, Wisdom & Grace*

*By Kim Groshek*

Courage stands when fear takes hold,
A heart of fire, a spirit bold.
Through storm and shadow, trial and test,
It beats within a fearless chest.

Wisdom walks where echoes fade,
A steady guide through light and shade.
Not in haste, but firm and true,
It sees beyond, it learns anew.

Grace, the whisper, soft yet strong,
A dance of kindness, righting wrongs.
Not in pride, nor seeking fame,
But lifting others in its name.

Together bound, these three remain,
Through loss, through love, through joy and pain.
With courage, step—no fear to chase,
With wisdom, walk—a steady pace,
And in all things, move with grace.

## *The Heart of It All*

*By Kim Groshek*

She wears many hats, but none for fame,
Her heart's the center, that's always the same.
She's the cook, the driver, the counselor too,
Yet somehow, she finds the time to renew.

Her hands are busy, her heart is full,
She gives, she gives, and never pulls.
In moments quiet, she stops and sighs,
Wondering if anyone realizes why.

But she won't ask, because she's been taught,
That love is given, never bought.
Her heart's the engine, the core, the soul,
The one thing that keeps it all whole.

Through sleepless nights and constant care,
She's there, she's always there.
Her heart beats louder than the rest,
For her, giving love is always best.

## *Return to Gold*

*By Kim Groshek*

The wardrobe waits, the journey ends,
But echoes hum where magic bends.
A Scarecrow bows, his mind now free,
The Tin Man feels, the Lion sees.
The girl in red, her heart still bold,
Steps once again on bricks of gold.
The road now bends to worlds unknown,
Yet courage marks the path she's sown.
In Lothlórien's golden light,
Galadriel gazes through the night.
Her mirror reflects what time can't steal—
The road ahead, the fate they feel.
For in the lands where legends fade,
The ring still glows, the debts are paid.
And where the Witch once cast her lies,
The dawn breaks bright in golden skies.
Gandalf stands, staff raised high,
The road unfolds beneath the sky.
He whispers, "The journey's never done,
The ring, the lion, the yellow sun."
For wisdom, heart, and courage rare,
Have written tales beyond compare.
And though the road winds evermore,
The Lion waits beyond the door.

## *Unlearning: 'Critical'*

*By Kim Groshek*

Start where you are,
Use what you have within,
Do what you can, now.

Then, it is unlearning,
To relearn, a new path,
Reflect on your thoughts.

First year at the university,
Struggles and stumbling blocks,
Yet, Critical Thinking emerged,
A skill for a lifetime forged.

Leadership competency,
A dance of confusion and clarity,
'Critical' versus true thinking,
Navigating the realms, unwinding.

Distinguish the difference,
Not 'criticizing', but understanding,
Ask questions, seek clarity,
In leadership's true capacity.

Step back from biases,
Objective inquiry,
Jonathon's tale unfolds,

Critical Thinking, a story told.

Assess the situation,
Beyond surface observations,
Uncover the system's play,
In the organizational ballet.

Evaluate, decide, act,
Leadership's critical pact,
A point of view, a plan,
Unlearn to understand.

Reflection in action,
The cycle of change,
In the dance of leadership,
Critical Thinking, rearrange.

Caveat to the wise,
Senior leaders introspect,
Before teaching, learn,
In your own system, detect.

I am a guide,
Navigating leadership's tide,
Unlearning for a future fair,
Critical Thinking, handle with care.

## *Build a Fortress of Wonder: Bathe in Its Glory*

*By Kim Groshek*

Living in a dream where time weaves its tale,
A garden of wisdom, whispered, unveiled.
No need to chase those butterflies, so bright,
Let your essence shine, a radiant light.

Butterflies flutter, wild and free,
Yet in your haven, they choose to be.
The fragrance of growth, colors of care,
Draw them in, on the soft summer air.

Chasing shadows, a quest that won't tire,
In self-cultivation, find your heart's desire.
Reflect in the mirror, embrace what's true,
For what you are, is what you will pursue.

A symphony of whispers, the universe sings,
Your authenticity, a melody that brings
The dreams you envision, the love you seek,
Not in chasing but in the soul's mystique.

Let your heart be a compass, spirit a guide,
In the tranquil orchard, where dreams coincide.
In the stillness of self-love's refrain,
All you long for, gently, will reign.

Don't chase the echoes, the transient flight,

Build a haven of wonder, bathe in its light.
Butterflies, captivated, linger and stay,
In the garden of your being, where dreams find their way.

In the dance of desires, let patience unfold,
Life's tapestry is woven, a story told.
Each bloom you nurture, a promise grown,
A haven of presence, your seeds are sown.

In the twilight of dreams, where time weaves its tale,
A garden of wisdom, whispered, unveiled.
No longer chase those elusive butterflies so bright,
Let your essence blaze, a radiant light.

In the dance of desires, let patience unfold,
Life's tapestry woven, a story untold.
Each bloom you nurture, a promise grown,
A sanctuary of presence, your seeds are bravely sown.

Butterflies flutter, wild and free,
Yet, in your haven, they choose to be.
The fragrance of growth, colors of care,
Draw them in on the soft summer air.

Cease chasing shadows, a quest that won't tire,
In self-cultivation, fuel your heart's fire.
Reflect in the mirror, embrace what's true,
For what you are is what you will pursue.

A symphony of whispers, the universe sings,
Your authenticity, a melody that stings
The dreams you envision, the love you seek,
Not in chasing but in the soul's mystique.

Let your heart be a compass, spirit a guide,
In the tranquil orchard, where dreams coincide.
In the stillness of self-love's refrain,
All you long for, forcefully, will reign.

Don't chase the echoes, the transient flight,

Build a fortress of wonder, bathe in its light.
Butterflies, captivated, linger and stay,
In the fortress of your being, where dreams find their way.

## *The Quiet Battle*

*By Kim Groshek*

She fights battles no one can see,
Holding her ground so others are free.
Her days are long, her nights are short,
She's always in some quiet sort.

She's learning to let go of the weight,
But it's hard to stop when it's your fate.
She carries the hopes of all she loves,
Hoping for peace from the heavens above.

In the quiet moments when all seems still,
She wonders if she's done enough to fill
The dreams she holds deep in her chest,
While giving her best, she's put to the test.

Yet through it all, her heart stays strong,
She knows her love is where she belongs.
A quiet battle, every single day,
Fighting for those who can't find their way.

## *For When We Meet Again*

*By Kevin Andre Lindstrøm*

Though time may stretch its cruel and heavy hand,
And days may pass like shadows on the wall,
I'll hold this love as tightly as I stand,
A beacon shining through the bitter squall.

No court nor word can sever what we share;
Your faces live within my every dream.
Each tear I shed becomes a whispered prayer.

A promise that this pain is not supreme.
One day, the tides will turn; the winds will shift,
And justice will restore what's been undone.
Until that day, my heart remains adrift,

But anchored still to you, my moon and sun.
For love endures where darkness cannot stay;
I'll find you when the clouds are swept away.

# *Part-5: Her Legacy*

## *Through Her Eyes*

*By Kim Groshek*

In her eyes, you'll see your worth,
A love that gives you endless birth.
She watches as you grow and rise,
Her love reflected in your eyes.

Through every storm, she stands with you,
Her faith in you, pure and true.
Her lessons deep, her heart so kind,
A mother's love, you'll always find.

Through triumphs and through days of rain,
She teaches how to love through pain.
Her hands, though worn, will never tire,
Her love will always lift you higher.

And when you leave, her love stays near,
A quiet force, a voice so clear.
Through her eyes, you'll always see,
A mother's love, eternally.

## *In Her Footsteps*

*By Kim Groshek*

She walks in footsteps worn by years,
Through every laugh, through every tear.
She learned to live through love's demand,
And now she walks, hand in hand.

She balances the weight of every task,
Without a second thought, no need to ask.
Her strength is silent, yet so loud,
A mother's love, forever proud.

She's given her best through all she's faced,
Never looking back, never out of place.
Her heart is home, a place of peace,
A love that never asks for release.

Her footsteps echo through the years,
A trail of love that calms all fears.
In her journey, her heart leads the way,
Guiding others through each new day.

## *A Prayer for Her Strength*

*By Kim Groshek*

God, hear my prayer for the woman I adore,
The one whose strength is like the ocean's roar.
She stands tall, even when she's tired,
Her heart fueled by love, never expired.

Grant her power when she feels weak,
A reminder that her heart will speak.
She's the warrior, the one who fights,
Help her find courage through the nights.

May her spirit never break or bend,
But find the strength to rise again.
For she's your daughter, a force untamed,
With every trial, she'll remain the same.

## *A Meditation for Her Love*

*By Kim Groshek*

Feel the warmth of your love unfold,
A gift so deep, so pure, so bold.
Close your eyes, take a breath of grace,
Feel the love in this sacred space.

You give so much, and yet you shine,
Your heart's a light, forever divine.
In every moment, you nurture and care,
Know that this love is always there.

As you meditate, breathe in the truth,
You are enough, from your youth to your proof.
Embrace your love, let it fill your soul,
For you, dear mother, make us whole.

## *The Heartbeat of Us*

*by Kim Groshek*

We rise together, though apart we stand,
Two mothers, side by side, hand in hand.
Our hearts beat with the same love, the same song,
In this sacred bond, we both belong.

Through every joy and every test,
We share this journey, we give our best.
So, dear mother, here's my heart to yours,
In this journey of love, our spirits soar.

## *Her Journey*

*By Kim Groshek*

She didn't choose this path at first,
But it's one she's walked with love and thirst.
For purpose, for joy, for all that's real,
She'll keep pushing forward, that's the deal.

She's walked through fear, through endless doubt,
Wondering if she'll figure it out.
But every step, she takes in stride,
Trusting that love will be her guide.

Her journey's long, but she's not alone,
She's built a family, carved her own throne.
Her heart is the compass, it never sways,
It leads her through the darkest of days.

She doesn't ask for applause or fame,
But her strength, her love, will always remain.
Her journey is one of love so pure,
Her heart the answer, always sure.

## *There is a Truth*

*By Dr. (hc) Verlaine Crawford*

"There is a truth beyond all truth,
a Wisdom that flows through the ages,
which carries with it the knowing that we are One.
Yet, there is sadness in parting from those we love,
a sadness in losing contact physically and mentally.
Elaine was a grand woman of great courage,
an orphan who created a loving home.
She gave her heart, love, care, and concern,
representing the splendid goddess of motherhood..."

## *Healing*

*By Kim Groshek*

Self-love, a journey profound,
A mystic healer on the spiritual ground.
Breakthroughs aplenty, understanding unfolds,
Transformative tales, as acceptance molds.

Sacred space, where healing begins,
Within ourselves, the magic spins.
Celebrate the essence, the light within,
Nurturing the soul, where self-love has been.

A dance with mystic hues, a healer's grace,
Paths intertwine in this sacred space.
The power of healing, an internal flow,
Embrace the journey, and let the self-love grow.

Spiritual breakthroughs, like whispers divine,
Choose your path, and let your spirit shine.
The connection deepens in the soul's embrace,
Self-love and growth, a harmonious grace.

## *In the Chaos*

*By Kim Groshek*

In the chaos, she finds her grace,
A soft smile upon her face.
Through endless calls and hurried tasks,
She gives her love, but never asks.

She balances dreams with the mundane,
Smiling through the joy and pain.
Her heart beats loud in the quiet of night,
Wishing for peace, hoping for light.

Her body may ache, her mind may tire,
But still, she presses on, never to retire.
She's the calm in the storm, the rock that stays,
Her love shining brightly through the haze.

So many things demand her time,
But she'll never stop—she'll always climb.
For in the chaos, she's still the one,
Who makes it all feel like it's just begun.

## *A Prayer Forgotten But Answered*

*By Randy Peyser*

Dear God, please heal my heart wherever it needs healing. It was a simple prayer, not the kind you'd expect to have lightning bolts thrown at.

Nor the kind that begs for mercy or the end to some horrific experience. It was just a simple prayer quietly whispered into the space of a languid afternoon.

There were no witnesses, not even the raised ear of a dog to note its mention. Nor was this prayer a dwelling place, like the one shouted daily that began with 'Please God' and ended with 'send me my soulmate.'

This was more like a slip of a prayer, briefly stated before it fell off the prayer pile, only to be quickly forgotten about. And here it was, just one week later, when she inquired:

'Do you like Vietnamese food?' It didn't matter. She insisted, and off we sped in a moldy Subaru never meant to hold legs longer than ski poles. Ten minutes later, the only parking place left in San Francisco was ours.

As I gulped down the last bite of pho, my companion headed toward the exit. Why the hurry?

Tip tossed down, I flung the door open to catch up with her outside.

And there stood a man. 'Hello, Randy.' Who was this man? My mind raced like a ticker tape.

Wait a minute. Those eyes. Holy shit! I know those eyes. Eleven years ago, and 3,500 miles across the country, I'd loved those eyes and the man who wore them.

It was Bruce, the great love of my life, the man who had asked me to marry him. The man who I was supposed to grow old with.

The same man who shattered my dreams into tiny splinters dotted with the furtive longings of unmet expectations. Here he was, eleven years later, on the opposite coast, in the doorway of a restaurant, and only a week after I'd gently asked to heal my heart with whoever I needed to heal it with.

We spoke for ten minutes. 'You know, I was just scared,' he said. And there it was, the reason Mr. Heartbreak had guillotined our relationship on my 28th birthday. And there it was, the closure I'd needed for eleven years finally happened.

Bruce drifted off into the life that was his, and my friend whisked me away in her moldy Subaru. At 28, he had been my true love. Eleven years later, he was merely a shadow who just happened to know my name.

You know, life doesn't always play out the way you imagine. Hearts break, and sometimes they never come back together again. But if a prayer half-forgotten can be answered, in spite of eleven years and 3,500 miles, perhaps next time, I will whisper a different prayer."

## *Generation Gaps*

*By Kim Groshek*

We're all talking, but are we listening?
The world's moving fast, but we're still missing
the beats that matter, the lessons of old,
the wisdom that doesn't fit into the mold.

We've got dreams that burn, and fires to start,
but sometimes forget to ask where to chart.
The past's got some answers, though we might not agree,
we need to pause and see what's meant to be.

The older voices speak in steady tones,
with stories we push to the background, alone.
But if we just stop, take a minute, take a breath,
we'll find we're connected in ways we've yet to accept.

We're not so different, you and me,
our struggles and triumphs are just as we see.
The gap's not a wall—it's a chance to align,
so let's bridge it together, redefine our time.

It's not about "them" or "us," it's all about "we,"
finding the balance, and setting it free.
The future's bright when we stand side by side,
building on what's old while we take new strides.

## *A Mother's Heart*

*By Murween Perry-Rose*

A mother comforts her child from the evening dawn,
Till sunlight shines, with gentle grace.
She nurtures love, a warm embrace,
Her heart is like gold, pure and bright,
Guiding through the darkest night.

She shows up when you slow down,
And there to kneel before the throne.
In every smile, in every tear,
In every challenge, she whispers dear.
Dispels all doubts and hearts of fear,
With every prayer, she spreads her love, beyond compare.

Her strength, her faith, her prayer—
A rock in stormy seas.
Her presence brings a calm serene of peace.
A mother's heart, a gift of love and grace.

## *Bridging Time: The Dance of Young Hearts and Old Souls*

*By Kim Groshek*

A whisper of wisdom, a call to be heard,
Across the vast gap where silence occurred.
The youth, full of fire, ignite their own dreams,
While the elders, with patience, flow like slow streams.
The world spins anew, but the stories stay true,
Old lessons, forgotten, yet waiting for you.
Bridging the gap, both the young and the wise,
To understand, to listen, to open our eyes.

One seeks the future, bright and unknown,
The other reflects on seeds that were sown.
In the clash of their voices, a harmony calls,
We rise together or we both take the fall.
But there's beauty in contrast, in rhythm and rhyme,
A dance of two generations, a balance of time.
For we all have a role in this tapestry grand,
Guiding each other with a gentle hand.

So pause, and listen—young hearts, old souls,
The wisdom of time makes us all whole.
A bridge is not built by just one side,
It's the joining of hands that teaches us pride.

## *Behind the Smile*

*By Kim Groshek*

Behind the smile is a heart that's full,
Of dreams, of love, and moments dull.
She doesn't show the weight she bears,
But inside, it's a constant affair.

She juggles it all with quiet grace,
Hoping no one sees her pace.
Her heart beats fast, her mind won't stop,
But she'll always rise, no matter how high the drop.

She's a warrior in every way,
Fighting for those who cannot say,
The dreams they hold, the things they need,
And she gives, she gives, with unmatched speed.

Behind the smile is a force so strong,
A love that's carried her all along.
Her heart is endless, it's full of light,
It's the reason she keeps up the fight.

## *The Quirky Survivor*

*By Tina Meeks*

"In Kensington's shadowed streets I grew,
Where childhood's innocence was far and few.
The 80s hummed with its neon glow,
Yet behind it, pain the world wouldn't show.

A nerd, a dreamer, odd to the eye,
The world would mock, and I'd wonder why.
Bullies sharpened their words like knives,
But I held tight to my inner lives.

Where others saw gray, I painted skies,
In my mind, a universe would rise.
The cracks in the pavement whispered tales,
Of survival, triumph, and setting sails.

I saw the world through a fractured lens,
Where hardship taught what kindness mends.
I faced what no child should have to see,
Yet in my difference, I found me.

Quirky, odd, unique, and bold,
A life of survival, a story told.
For in being strange, I found my grace—
A spark, a strength, no one could erase.

The world tried to break me, but I stood tall,

A data nerd who rose above it all.
Through struggle and fire, I learned to thrive,
And I'm proud that my difference kept me alive."

## *Reach for the Sky*

*By Kim Groshek*

Spotlight shine on dreams untamed.
The world is waiting, say your name
Feed our tapping hearts in sync
Tonight we rise on the brink

Energy surging through the air
Voices buzzing everywhere
The rhythm's bold, it lifts you high
An anthem shouting reach the sky

Feel the pulse, let it steer
Every moment starts right here
This is the spark, the grand debut
The stage is set, it's all for you

That's a line like gears in time
You're the spark, this peaks your climb
No holding back, the rush is real
The beat reflects the passion you feel

The countdown's ending, dreams ignite
Every second burns so bright
A wave of cheers, a tidal roar
This opening is what we're born for

Feel the pulse, let it steer

Every moment starts right here
This is the spark, the grand Debut
The stage is set, it's all for you

## *The Silent Hero*

*By Kim Groshek*

She's the hero no one sees,
Fighting battles on bended knees.
Her cape is worn, but still it flies,
Under the stars, beneath the skies.

She hides her tears, her fears so deep,
But for them, she'll never sleep.
She's the one who keeps the world turning,
While quietly her heart is yearning.

She's built a life out of love and care,
With no thought of what's fair.
Her strength is in the way she moves,
In every sacrifice, in every groove.

The silent hero, she's always there,
Unseen, yet beyond compare.
Her heart is her superpower,
It shines bright in every hour.

## *Song of Lost Time*

*By Menachem Rephun*

"You are the moon
(The sunlight is fading)
And the trees by the sea
(You stopped to reflect)

Were rocked by the wind
(The caress of your fingers)
Just the ghost of a memory
(Is all that you've left him)

Will be stirred to arise
(By the warmth of the sun)
In a season of sorrow
(The rain rushing down)

Will cover his body
(With the passing of Spring)
He will seek to forget you
(A return to the time)
And through the low valley
(He will lie down and dream)"

## *The Wild and the Wise*

*by Kim Groshek*

She wakes when the sun has climbed too high,
wrapped in blankets, a sigh, a sigh.
The world hums softly, waiting near,
but she drags her steps without much cheer.

Her sister, steady, pencil tight,
fingers dance in morning light.
Lists and plans and checkmarks too,
mapping out the days anew.

She stumbles down, a whirlwind bright,
blanket trailing, heart alight.
"Morning, world!" she sings with glee,
carefree steps, untamed and free.

But duty looms, a patient ghost,
whispering futures, firm and close.
Her sister sits with careful grace,
while she resists time's hurried chase.

Two halves of one, both bound yet free—
the wild, the wise, a harmony.

## *Her Heart, Her World*

*By Kim Groshek*

She's the heartbeat of every day,
The one who leads and shows the way.
She gives her all with each breath she takes,
For every smile, for every stake.

Her heart is full, her hands are tired,
But she's never lost, she's never retired.
She's built a world with all her love,
Guided by the stars above.

Through sleepless nights and endless work,
She'll never let her family shirk.
Her love's a light, her strength a song,
In her heart, they all belong.

She may be tired, but she'll never fall,
For she is the heart, the love of it all.
Her world is full, her love is wide,
And in her heart, they all reside.

## *You're Still Here*

*By Patricia Theriot*

"Mom, I took a hike today
To see the ocean from up high.
I have a lot I'd like to say
But still can't seem to say bye.

Water still wells when I think of the past
You seemed to fade extremely fast.
You seemed to have a golden hue
Your love was honest and pure and true.

I'm glad I was there at the end
But my heart has not begun to mend.
I'm up here and feel the wind on my face
I know you are with God, in a better place.

When I get there, we can walk the streets of gold.
And talk about every story untold.
I'm ok mom, I'm living a full life
I'm a friend, sister, mother, and wife.

Everything good I learned from you
You were our heart, our center, our glue.
I have days where I sob and it doesn't seem real
But it's ok to be sad, to hurt, and to feel.

Life keeps on going, so I will too
But thank you for everything, and I love you."

*Pancakes and Plans*

*by Kim Groshek*

She bounds into the kitchen late,
a cape of warmth, a twist of fate.
The scent of pancakes fills the air,
but work and whispers linger there.

Her sister sits, composed, refined,
a book in hand, a sharpened mind.
She chews in squares, precise and neat,
while She devours without retreat.

A job, they say, a plan to make,
a future firm, a path to take.
She groans, she slumps, she rolls her eyes,
why cage the heart when it can fly?

Her sister's dreams are crisp and clear,
while hers drift wide, unformed, sincere.
One maps life like a careful scheme,
the other dances in a dream.

Yet somewhere deep in laughter's glow,
a thread unites, though neither knows.

## *The Storms of Love*

*By Jaidei Pinder*

Okay
I've had enough!
And I don't know how to say this
nicely.

It may hurt, or it may surprise
but inside no longer can this hide!
I'm tired of being
Wrapped up in you, like a knitted sweater

When all I want to do is scream
Because I feel you should know better.
Is it a letter that you're waiting on?
I hope that's not the case because

The storms raging on the inside
Reminds me of abhorrent weather.
Like a hurricane,
with fierce winds howling on the outside

so, does my heart beat
When thoughts of you drift through my mind
Chiseling at my subconscious
You'd think I was stuck in a gold mine.

* * *

But I didn't know how long this storm will last
but you need to be a bit speedy with your response;
because if time was to have its way
I only have one thing to say and it's not going to be nice

But I'm tired of the wait and hopes the weight of this
Doesn't give you a heart attack, but make it known,
I'm not going to be waiting forever!"

## *Sisterhood in Summer*

*by Kim Groshek*

Sunlight spills through sleepy blinds,
She stirs but fights the waking signs.
The world outside is bright and new,
but dreams still hold their golden hue.

Her sister sits, all straight and tall,
a world contained within the scrawl.
She notes, she plans, she writes with grace,
while She resists time's hurried chase.

One structured tight, the other free,
but both entwined in history.
Through teasing words and pancake fights,
they balance days and endless nights.

The future calls, the past still sings,
but summer hums with simpler things.
Sisterhood in sunlit beams,
woven soft through childhood dreams.

## *Here*

*By Amanda Horton*

"wind harassing my tear-stained
cheeks. fog surrounding my exhausted
eyes. silence drowning out my deafening
thoughts. light dancing around my unspoken
hopes.

prayer covering my all encompassing grief.
Here. I stand.
Here. I recover.
Here. I heal."

## *Fragments of a Dream*

*by Kim Groshek*

Woke up breathless, tangled in sheets,
like I'd surfaced from something too deep to name.
Morning light too soft, too ordinary
for the way my heart slammed against my ribs.

I tried to trace the edges,
pull the dream back from the dark—
but it slipped,
a wisp of smoke between my fingers.

Only the panic remained,
its claws still in my throat.
And her sister.
Her sister was there, somehow.

## *Breakfast Conversations*

*by Kim Groshek*

Toast,
cold and stale,
crumbs scattering
like her patience.

Her dad's voice,
clipped precision,
her mom's touch,
too light to hold her still.

"Maybe help your sister," her mom says,
but all she hears is
*be better,*
*do more, be like her.*

They don't say it,
but she tastes it between bites.
She swallows hard,
the silence heavier than her words.

## *A Message to my Son*

*By April Randall*

Son, I have never lied to you and I will not start now. The truth of the matter is, I never wanted you to come around.
This is harsher than it sounds. The truth is, I was afraid I would not make you proud.

Raising a Black male in America, was the last thing I wanted to do. I am simply not equipped for the task and knew I would not last.
You deserve someone better than me. You deserve the sky and the sea and everything in between.

You light up my day, but haunt my nights. I close my eyes and I am instantly filled with fright. The world is not fair even though you are gifted and bright.
I fear for you and I pray for you. As I watch you grow, I realize there is so much I do not know.

I am sorry, son, that I am not the mother you need me to be. I am sorry that you sometimes see the worst parts of me.
I am sorry that I want to hold you so tight with all of my might and keep you beside me every single night.

Son, I am doing the best that I can. I wish I knew God's ultimate plan.
I do not have all of the answers or all of the skills, but there is one thing that I do have, and that is the will."

## *Between Sisters*

*by Kim Groshek*

Her sister watches her,
eyes full of warnings,
hands too small to hold her back.

"The quarry's dangerous," she says,
like she doesn't already know.
Like she doesn't crave the shock of cold water,
the rush that drowns out everything else.

Her sister worries like it's her job,
like she won't make it back.
But she was born to push limits,
to run before looking down.

Her sister doesn't get it.
She never will.
And maybe,
that's the rift growing between them.

## *Ode to a Galaxy*

*By Jenny Elinora*

"Yellow yellow yellow
a starburst, to say the least
first, the intense chemical reactions
then the inevitable light
promise and energy renewable over, over, again
I've got at least a billion more years in me at this rate."

## *Hymn of Nature*

*By Kim Groshek*

Oh, blessed is the one who walks
Through forests deep where silence talks,
Where rivers carve the earth with grace,
And sunlight warms each sacred space.

She wanders where wildflowers rise,
A canvas brushed by endless skies,
Where mountains stand in solemn might,
And eagles trace the edge of light.

No hands of man, no city's gleam,
Can match the wonder of a stream,
Or whisper truth as clear and free
As wind that moves the ancient tree.

The waves still call, the meadows hum,
A language pure, where lies are none.
For nature holds no false disguise,
Its beauty shines, its wisdom guides.

Truth is woven in the land,
In shifting tides, in grains of sand.
It does not bend, it does not break,
It stands in all the world we wake.

* * *

So pause, look close, and you will see—
The voice of truth in sky and sea.
For in the light, the storm, the stone,
Lies something greater than our own.

## *The Weight of Words*

*By Kim Groshek*

The words sit heavy in your chest, don't they?
Like stones in deep water, sinking slow,
Pressing, waiting, whispering secrets,
How long have you carried their weight below?

They linger in pauses, in laughter's hush,
In the quiet before the world takes flight,
Shadows of echoes, memories unspoken,
Ghosts that dance in the hush of night.

But what if—just what if—you set them free?
Let them spill like light through a shattered seam,
Let them weave into someone's silence,
A tether, a bridge, a mended dream.

Write them, speak them, let them rise,
Let them echo beyond the fear inside,
For somewhere, someone needs your story—
And so do you—no need to hide.

## *Threads of Time*

*By Kim Groshek*

Hand in hand, through years we weave,
A story only love can leave.
You, my guide—soft yet strong,
A melody, my lifelong song.

Eyes that sparkle, old and wise,
Holding echoes, ancient skies.
A heart that whispers, calm and true,
Teaching me what love can do.

Through storms and light, you show the way,
With words unspoken, yet loud they stay.
Not just a mother, but soul's embrace,
A mirror of grace, a timeless place.

So as we walk this path anew,
Know my heart beats because of you.
A daughter, a mother—woven tight,
Two old souls, forever light.

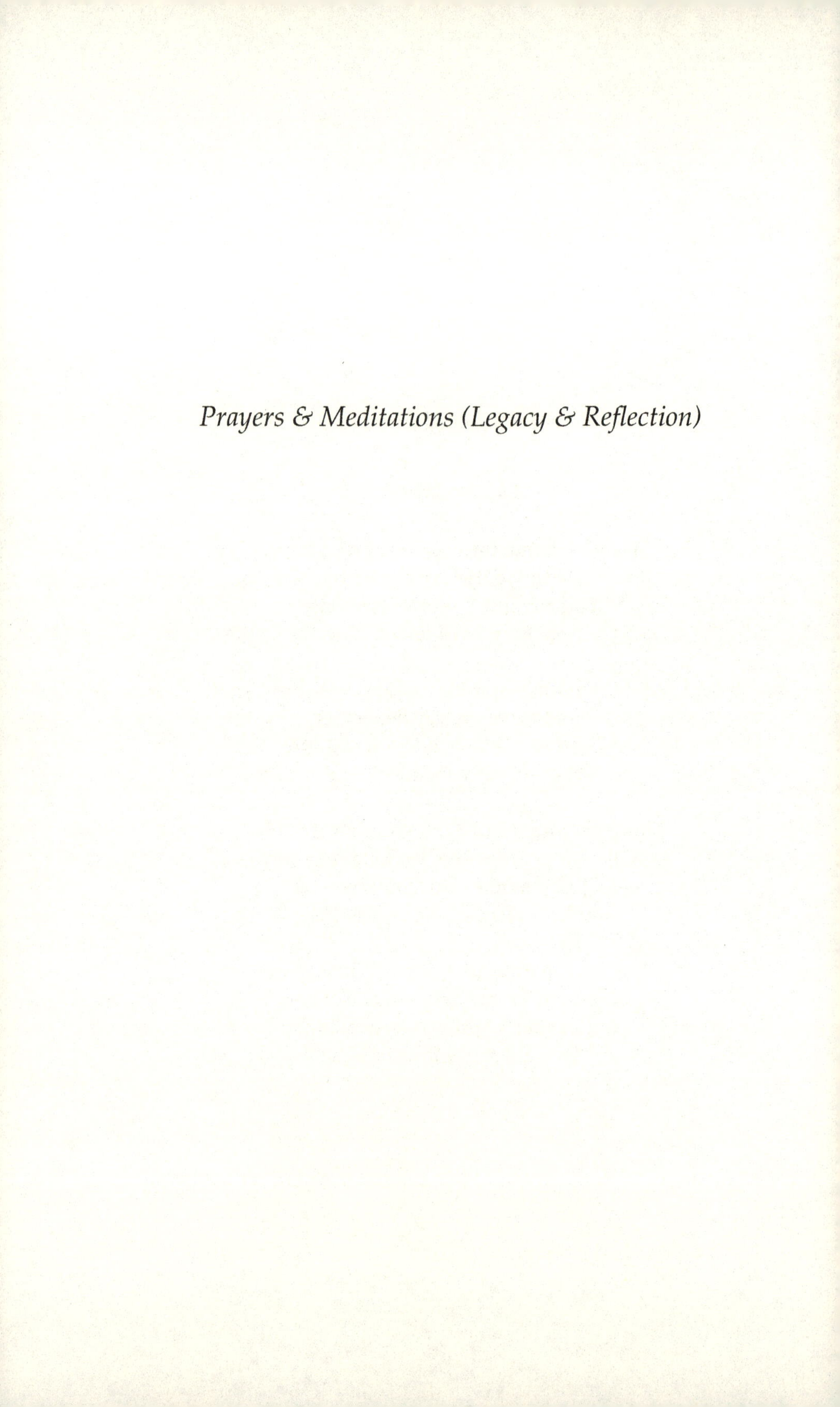

*Prayers & Meditations (Legacy & Reflection)*

## *A Prayer for Her Peace*

*By Kim Groshek*

In the quiet of this morning's light,
I lift a prayer, a soft, gentle flight.
For my mother, whose love runs deep,
I ask for peace, as she wakes from sleep.

May she find stillness amidst the noise,
A moment of calm to simply rejoice.
Grant her heart rest and gentle grace,
In every step, in every place.

Let her feel the love she's given,
Reflect back to her, a light from heaven.
In this moment, I pray for her,
That peace and strength may always occur.

## *A Meditation for Her Soul*

*By Kim Groshek*

Breathe deeply, mother, and let it go,
The worries that endlessly flow.
Let your heart rest, let your mind be still,
In this moment, find your will.

You are the sun that lights our days,
In every storm, you find your ways.
May your soul feel light and free,
As you meditate on what is meant to be.

Release the burdens, feel the ease,
In your spirit, find your peace.
You are enough, in all you do,
A soul so strong, so pure, so true.

## *A Meditation for Her Journey*

*By Kim Groshek*

Sit quietly, mother, and listen to your heart,
In this stillness, you're a work of art.
You've journeyed far, but there's more to go,
Let this moment heal, let your spirit glow.

Visualize the road ahead, winding and wide,
Know that with every step, you're guided with pride.
You've faced so much, and yet you rise,
A mother's strength is her greatest prize.

Take a breath, feel the peace you deserve,
You've nurtured all with an endless curve.
In this moment, feel grounded and true,
The universe supports everything you do.

## *A Prayer for Her Rest*

*By Kim Groshek*

Tonight, I lift a prayer for you,
May you find rest, as dreams come through.
For all the work you've done today,
Let peace surround you, come what may.

You've given so much, more than you know,
It's time for you to let your spirit flow.
Sleep, dear mother, with a heart at ease,
May your soul feel light, like the gentle breeze.

I pray for restful sleep tonight,
May your dreams be calm, your heart be light.
In the morning, when the sun does rise,
May peace and strength fill your eyes.

## *A Prayer for Her Courage*

*By Kim Groshek*

Oh, Lord, grant her courage today,
To face whatever comes her way.
She's been strong, she's fought so long,
Help her remember she's where she belongs.

In moments of doubt, lift her high,
Let her heart soar like the endless sky.
Grant her the power to stand and be,
The brave, bold woman she's meant to be.

Let her feel your strength in her veins,
For courage is born in the deepest pains.
With every challenge, she will rise,
For her spirit is fierce, and love never dies.

## *A Meditation for Her Heart*

*By Kim Groshek*

In this quiet moment, mother, rest,
Let go of all that weighs your chest.
Breathe deeply, feel the love inside,
The endless light you can't hide.

Your heart beats strong, steady, and true,
With every beat, you are renewed.
In every sigh, in every prayer,
Know that you're held in love and care.

As you meditate, let your heart soar,
You've given so much, but there's more.
In this stillness, find your grace,
And feel the love you've given embrace.

## *A Prayer for Her Peace of Mind*

*By Kim Groshek*

Dear Lord, grant her peace of mind,
A gift so rare, so hard to find.
In the rush of life, the constant spin,
Let calm surround her from within.

When worries cloud her thoughtful eyes,
Lift her soul and clear the skies.
Let her know, with every breath,
That peace is hers, beyond all death.

In moments still, grant her release,
So she may rest and find her peace.
With every prayer, with every sigh,
May calmness fall from the endless sky.

## *A Meditation for Her Soul's Purpose*

*By Kim Groshek*

Mother, take a moment to breathe,
To let go of all that you grieve.
Feel the purpose that fills your soul,
The love you give, the ways you roll.

You are more than the roles you play,
You are a light, a guide, a ray.
Let your soul rise to the stars,
For you've always been, and will always are.

In this moment, know your worth,
You're a treasure beyond this earth.
As you meditate, feel the truth,
Your purpose is love, and that's the proof.

# *Closing Thoughts*

## *The Strength We Share*

*by Kim Groshek*

In quiet moments, when the world is loud,
We stand as warriors, heads unbowed.
The weight of love, heavy yet light,
We carry it all, through day and night.

Your heart is tender, yet so strong,
In this sisterhood, we both belong.
So let us pause and share this grace,
For we're all mothers in this sacred space.

## *Hands That Hold*

*by Kim Groshek*

Your hands have held dreams, hopes, and tears,
Guided through joy and conquered fears.
Like mine, they've rocked, soothed, and prayed,
Holding our children in a love never swayed.

Though our paths differ, we share the same song,
Of giving our all and carrying on.
Know that in your heart, there's a place for me,
For we're both mothers, in unity.

## *In the Quiet of Our Hearts*

*by Kim Groshek*

In the quiet of the night, when the stars take their place,
We hold our children close, in a tender embrace.
The world may not see, nor always understand,
The depth of our love, as we walk hand in hand.

So, dear mother, when doubt clouds your view,
Know I stand with you, strong and true.
Through the sleepless nights and endless days,
We find strength in each other's ways.

*A Prayer for You, A Prayer for Me*

*by Kim Groshek*

I pray for you, as I pray for me,
For patience, grace, and strength to be.
May your heart stay open, kind and free,
As you walk this journey, just like me.

Through every trial, every tear,
May love light the path that draws you near.
And when the days feel long and steep,
Know that in sisterhood, our hearts will keep.

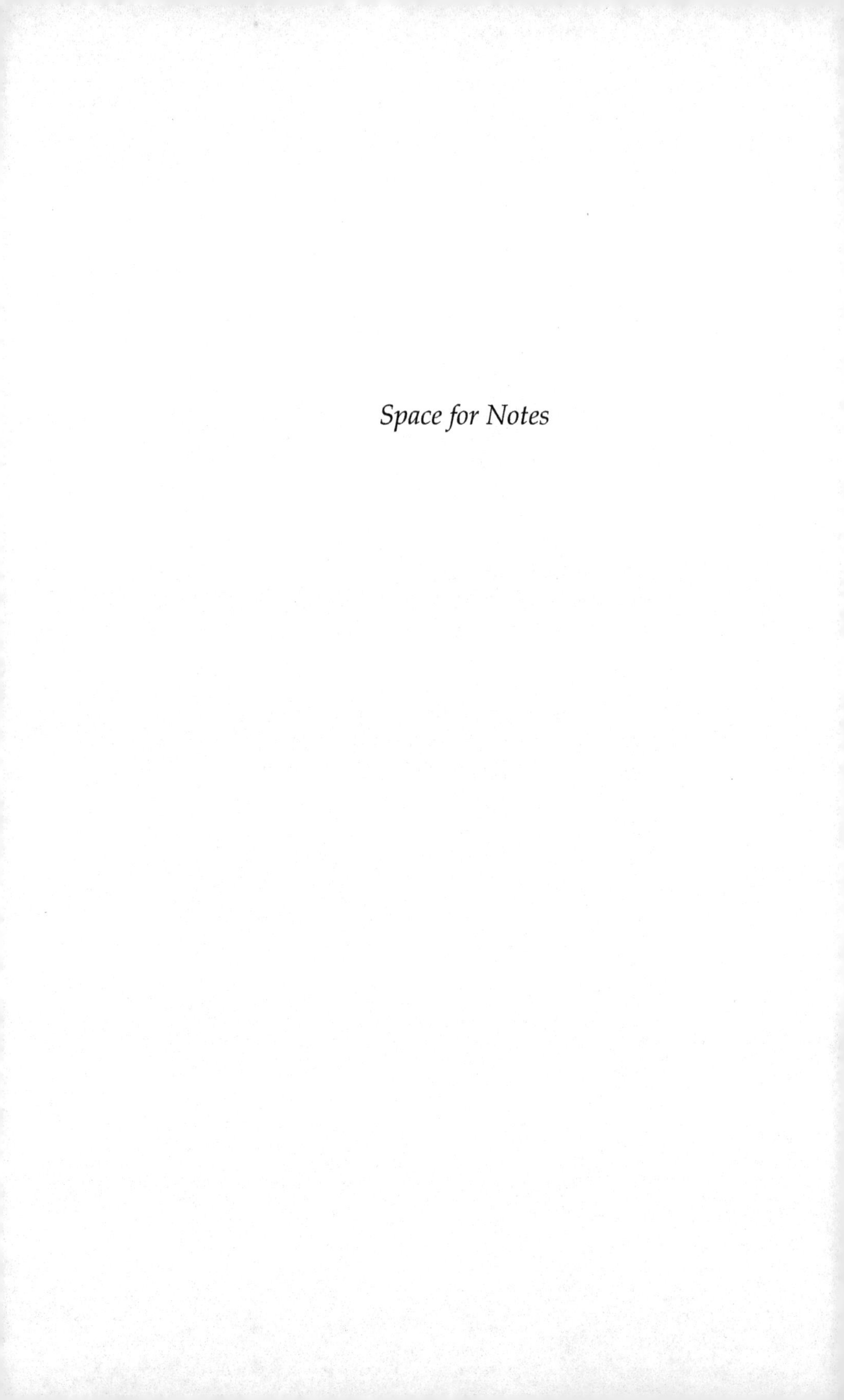

*Space for Notes*

# *Epilogue*

*From the Heart of Kim Groshek*
We hope our sweet melodies linger in your heart,
like whispered lullabies carried by the wind,
soft, yet powerful—woven with love,
meant to embrace, to heal, to remind.

May these words be a gentle pause,
a moment of warmth in your soul's embrace.
For every step we take, every breath we hold,
is a verse in the song of love and grace.

As you carry these echoes forward,
may they ring in your heart like a timeless tune,
guiding you home to the beauty within—
where love never fades and light forever blooms.

With love, Kim Groshek

*With Love!*

Put this book by your bedside table and read it again and again.